YOUR KNOWLEDGE HAS VALUE

- We will publish your bachelor's and master's thesis, essays and papers

- Your own eBook and book - sold worldwide in all relevant shops

- Earn money with each sale

Upload your text at www.GRIN.com and publish for free

Micha Schlittenhardt

Intercultural competence: general or specific?

Can the concept of cohesion also be seen as a specific-orientated approach of intercultural competence?

GRIN Verlag

Bibliografische Information der Deutschen Nationalbibliothek:

Die Deutsche Bibliothek verzeichnet diese Publikation in der Deutschen National-
bibliografie; detaillierte bibliografische Daten sind im Internet über http://dnb.d-
nb.de/ abrufbar.

Imprint:

Copyright © 2012 GRIN Verlag GmbH
Druck und Bindung: Books on Demand GmbH, Norderstedt Germany
ISBN: 978-3-656-59151-1

This book at GRIN:

http://www.grin.com/en/e-book/268140/intercultural-competence-general-or-spe-
cific

GRIN - Your knowledge has value

Der GRIN Verlag publiziert seit 1998 wissenschaftliche Arbeiten von Studenten, Hochschullehrern und anderen Akademikern als eBook und gedrucktes Buch. Die Verlagswebsite www.grin.com ist die ideale Plattform zur Veröffentlichung von Hausarbeiten, Abschlussarbeiten, wissenschaftlichen Aufsätzen, Dissertationen und Fachbüchern.

Visit us on the internet:

http://www.grin.com/

http://www.facebook.com/grincom

http://www.twitter.com/grin_com

CAN THE CONCEPT OF COHESION ALSO BE SEEN AS A SPECIFIC-ORIENTATED
APPROACH OF INTERCULTURAL COMPETENCE?
Essay by Micha Ulrich Schlittenhardt

The debate on the concept of Intercultural Competence became a wide field of interest in recent years which could be especially seen on the discourse in the German-speaking world (Cf. Bolton, 2006; Rathje 2007). Furthermore, it gained importance in society due to the development towards an intercultural society in Germany and the question for integration (Cf. Seifert 2012). Business sector and governments are therefore in search for Intercultural Competence in order to counter these issues (ibid.).

THE DEVELOPMENT OF AN INTERCULTURAL COMPETENCE CONSTRUCT
To define the construct of Intercultural Communication different approaches were made. Beginning with the **list model** of three major dimension: *affective*, therefore depending on the capability of adaption and the individual personality; *conative*, depending on situational behavior and communication, and the *cognitive* dimension (Cf. Gertsen 1990). These lay foundation to the development of models to accommodate the construct of Intercultural Communication. The **structural model** (Cf. Bolton, 2006) of Intercultural Communication, containing the aforementioned dimensions based on personal capability towards a **situational based** (Cf. Thomas, 2003) counter model. Both find their conclusion in an **interaction model** of Intercultural Competence, where situation, through context, and personality play a major role. Furthermore, the model of **Cultural Intelligence** tries to conclude these frameworks to a model of the capability of adaption in a specific situation. Moreover, can this construct be set into three different levels on which the construct is depending: the motivational level, the level of action and the level of reflection.

These approaches inherit the predominant coherence-based definition of culture, which describes the interaction between two differing cultures as an intercultural frame and therefore gives name to the concept. By seeing the personality of the individual as culturally based in respect of a coherence-based *foundation*, Intercultural Competence has to be examined in a cultural specific *scope*.

A COUNTER APPROACH AND THE DEFINITION OF CULTURE

Rathje (2007) reflects the debate in the German-speaking world by joining the discourse of Intercultural Communication by stating strategic questions on the *goal*, the *scope*, the *application* and the *foundation* of an Intercultural Communication concept. Furthermore, suggests Rathje (2007) a cohesion-based approach, which is described as multi-collectivistic view on culture that forms the individual culture of a person. Caused by this radical individualistic culture (Cf. Rathje, 2009), similarities can be found between the two interacting individuals. Therefore, the interaction cannot be seen as an intercultural framework but rather as intercommunity. If only similarities are the key to Intercultural Competence, a general scope is found.

In view of this two stated approaches on the definition of culture and interaction between parties, the following questions are raised: *Is the cohesion-based approach only applicable on a general-scope? Can the concept of cohesion also be seen as a specific-orientated approach of intercultural competence? Is there only one valid approach?*

THE CLASSICAL APPROACH AS SPECIFIC SCOPE

The coherence-based definition of culture gives a raw outline on the discourse on the definition of culture in recent decades. In sight of the construct of Intercultural Competence, culture is defined as differently coherent collectives, therefore an exclusive system. This makes it facile to summarize cultural differences by organizing them into different niches and giving them a catalogue of explications, such as the Iceberg or the Onion-model (Cf. Hofstede 2011). These models help to understand enclosed culture in general and determine specific rules for interaction in an intercultural encounter between two differing cultures or collectives. However, these models used in a macro perspective can also be seen as description of an individual culture and therefore give only raw insight on a national culture, which could differ in its elements.

Moreover, the classical approach of coherence led to the reduction of culture itself, for example in educational literature, by stereotyping the national cultures. Even when stereotypes support a person to prepare for an intercultural encounter, the stereotype can be misleading due to the overstatement of stereotypes into a list of rules and habits that have to be adapted even if the counterpart differs from the own collectively seen culture.

This issue in the definition of culture, and furthermore, the concept of Intercultural Competence is met by the cohesion-based approach.

THE COHESION-BASED APPROACH AS ANSWER

As stated before, is the cohesion-based model the outcome of multi-collectivism, which implies the presence of an individual in different collectives. Therefore, the individual is able to adapt different habits and rules from differing collectives in which he or she takes part and forms a radical individual culture due to the collectives the individual is into. If the individual have an encounter with another, he or she should be able to find similarities of habits or rules to determine them in the own definition as individual culture. This gives a general scope to the Intercultural Competence construct.

Due to the connection between collectives, where individuals play the linking point, a connection to the counter culture should be found and serve as connection between the encountering parties in intercommunity. Differences therefore appear as familiar and normal due to the experience made in different collectives and cultural notions.

This approach seems like an answer to the issue of Intercultural Competence and reflects a general scope on this construct, which would serve perfectly for Intercultural Competence training. But, in case of no connection between any of the collectives between the acting individuals, this concept would lack. Furthermore, this case, in a sterilized point of view, would mean again an intercultural encounter of two differing cultures, and therefore require a culture-specific scope as the case gives a coherence image.

THE RIGHT BALANCE

Therefore, a right balance hast to be found in order to meet the general and specific scope. No scope could exist without the other; both are required for Intercultural Competence. A general scope could mean to find connectors first and second to adept specifically in an in-depth step of interaction. Furthermore, it can be stated that a macro perspective could mean a general-based cohesion model of culture followed by a specific-based coherence-model. Both are needed to meet the requirements in an intercultural encounter.

In conclusion it can be stated that the scope is always a question of definition and perspective. The right balance has to be granted and efforts have to be made to find a suitable definition of culture and Intercultural Competence which fit the approaches made. Also studies on coherence- and cohesion-based definitions should be made in order to develop a scientific falsified holistic theory on cultural definition which includes a macro and micro perspective on culture. Still this question remain: *Will there ever be a holistic model?*

Literature

Bolten, J. (2006): Interkulturelle Kompetenz. In: L.R. Tsuasman (Ed.): Das große Lexikon Medien und Kommunikation , pp. 163-166. Würzburg: Ergon.

Gertsen, M.C. (1990): Intercultural competence and expatriates. In: The international Journal of Human Resource Management 1(3), pp. 341-362.

Hofstede, G. (2011): Lokales Denken, globales Handeln: Interkulturelle Zusammenarbeit und globales Management. DTV-Beck (5).

Rathje, S. (2007): Intercultural Competence: The Status and Future of a Controversial Concept. In: Language and Intercultural Communication 7 (4), pp. 254-266.

Rathje, S. (2009): Der Kulturbegriff - Ein anwendungsorientierter Vorschlag zur Generalüberholung. In: Konzepte kultureller Differenz – Münchener Beiträge zur interkulturellen Kommunikation. München.

Thomas, A. (2003): Interkulturelle Kompetenz: Grundlagen, Probleme und Konzepte. In: Erwägen, Wissen, Ethik 14 (1), pp. 137-221.

Seifert, J. (2012): Umdenken bei der Integration. In: Welt Online, http://www.welt.de/print/die_welt/hamburg/article106274662/Umdenken-bei-der-Integration.html (last accessed 06/05/12).